A Note to Parents

D0205663

DK READERS is a compelling new program
for beginning readers, designed in conjunction with
leading literacy experts, including Dr. Linda Gambrell,
Director of the School of Education at Clemson
University. Dr. Gambrell has served on the Board of
Directors of the International Reading Association and
as President of the National Reading Conference.

Beautiful illustrations and superb full-color
photographs combine with engaging, easy-to-read stories
to offer a fresh approach to each subject in the series.
Each DK READER is guaranteed to capture a child's
interest while developing his or her reading skills, general
knowledge, and love of reading.

The four levels of DK READERS are aimed at
different reading abilities, enabling you to choose
the books that are exactly right for your child:

Level 1 – Beginning to read
Level 2 – Beginning to read alone
Level 3 – Reading alone
Level 4 – Proficient readers

The "normal" age at which a child
begins to read can be anywhere from
three to eight years old, so these
levels are only a general guideline.

No matter which level you
select, you can be sure that you
are helping your child learn to
read, then read to learn!

LONDON, NEW YORK, MUNICH,
MELBOURNE, and DELHI

Project Editor Naia Bray-Moffatt,
Art Editor Catherine Goldsmith
Managing Editor Bridget Gibbs
US Editor Regina Kahney
Senior Art Editor Clare Shedden
Senior DTP Designer Bridget Roseberry
Production Shivani Pandey
Jacket Designer Karen Burgess
Indexer Lynn Bresler
Photographer John Daniels

Reading Consultant
Linda Gambrell, Ph.D.

First American Edition, 2001
03 04 05 10 9 8 7 6 5 4 3 2
Published in the United States by DK Publishing, Inc.
375 Hudson Street, New York, New York 10014

Copyright © 2001 Dorling Kindersley Limited, London

All rights reserved under International and Pan-American
Copyright Conventions. No part of this publication
may be reproduced, stored in a retrieval system,
or transmitted in any form or by any means, electronic,
mechanical, photocopying, recording, or otherwise, without
the prior written permission of the copyright owner.

Published in Great Britain by Dorling Kindersley Limited.

Library of Congress Cataloging-in-Publication Data
Hayden, Kate.
    Pony show / by Kate Hayden. -- 1st American ed.
        p. cm. -- (Dorling Kindersley readers)
    ISBN 0-7894-7371-2 (pbk) ISBN 0-7894-7372-0 (hc)
    1. Show riding--Juvenile literature. 2. Show ponies--Juvenile
literature. 3. Horsemanship--Juvenile literature. 1. Show riding.
2. Horsemanship. 3. Show ponies. 4. Ponies.]
I. Title. II. Series.
SF295.2 .H39 2001
798.2'4--dc21   00-056975

Additional photography: Andy Crawford,
Kit Hougton, Bob Langrish, Stephen Oliver

Models: Linda Cannon, Lucy Cannon,
Tom Cannon and Emma McAllister
All other images © Dorling Kindersley Limited.
For further information see: www.dkimages.com

Color reproduction by Colourscan, Singapore
Printed and bound in China by L. Rex Printing Co., Ltd.

see our complete product line at

www.dk.com

DK READERS

Horse Show

Written by Kate Hayden

DK Publishing, Inc.

It's a busy afternoon
at White Lane Farm.
Lucy, Emma, and Tom
are cleaning saddles and bridles
for the horse show tomorrow.

Maggie Cole is their riding teacher.
She is pleased to see the shiny tack.
"Good job, everyone!" she says.
"Now let's go and say goodnight
to the horses."

Tack

A horse's leather saddle
and bridle are called tack.
Tack must be cleaned
often to keep the leather
soft and to look good.

Lucy's favorite horse is called Lady.

Lady is a Welsh Mountain pony.

She's small but very strong.

Lucy will be riding Lady tomorrow.

Food
Hay and fresh
drinking water are
needed to keep a
horse fit and healthy.

Before Lucy goes home,
she checks that Lady has
enough hay and water.
She strokes Lady's nose
and pats her neck.
"Goodnight, Lady.
See you in
the morning."

There are four other horses
at White Lane Farm.

Sid is a tiny Shetland.
He gives rides
to little children.

Candy is a frisky young chestnut.
She is a good jumper
but hard to handle.

Bingo is a
gentle Pinto.
He will be
Tom's horse
at the show.

Twinkle is a
quiet New Forest pony.
He is a good horse for beginners.
Emma is glad she'll be riding
Twinkle tomorrow.

Lucy, Emma, and Tom arrive
at the stables early the next day.
There is lots to do before the show.

First Aid
A horse that is limping
must not be ridden. A
first aid kit may be used
to treat minor injuries,
or a vet may be called.

First they bring the horses
out into the yard to groom them.
"Oh no," says Tom.
"Bingo's limping."
"We'll have to take
Candy instead," says Maggie.
"Don't worry. You can handle her."

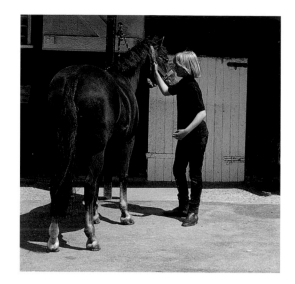

Lucy uses a body brush
on Lady's coat and mane.
Then she washes Lady's tail
and puts it in a bandage
to keep it tidy.

Grooming
Regular grooming by
cleaning, combing,
and brushing keeps
a horse's coat looking
shiny and healthy.

Tom cleans out Candy's hooves
with a hoof pick.
She keeps nipping at his shirt.
Tom tells her to keep still.
"And don't bite."
Maggie talks to Candy gently
to calm her down.

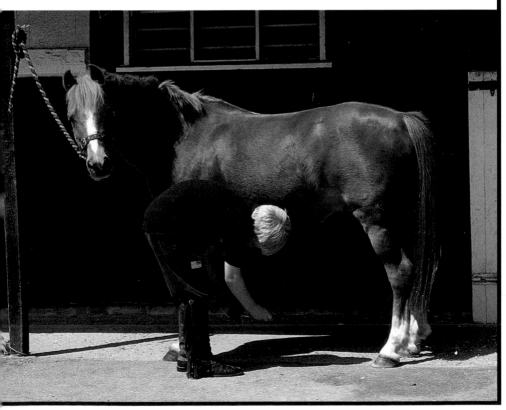

Now it's time to load the horses
into the horsebox.
Lady and Twinkle
go in quietly
but Candy stops
and refuses to budge.

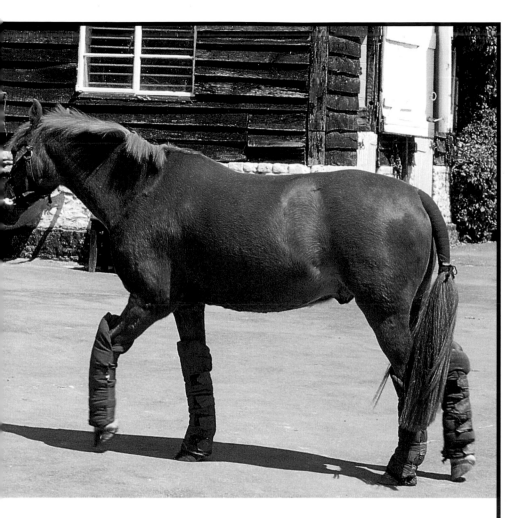

"I wish you were good, like Bingo,"
says Tom.
"Try giving her a bit of apple,"
says Maggie.
The apple works!
Soon, Candy is safely on board.

At the show ground
the children bring the horses out
and tether them to the horsebox.
The children have changed
into their riding clothes.

Riding Hat
Hard hats must be
worn when riding to
protect the rider's
head if he or she falls
off the horse.

The horses need a warm up
before the show.
But Tom has trouble
getting on to Candy.
She's very excited
and won't stay still.

Emma is about to take part in the
Walk, Trot, and Canter event.
She knows Twinkle
will behave well.
Emma sits up straight in the saddle.
Maggie checks her position.
"Relax your shoulders and hands,"
she says.
"Hold the reins lightly
so they don't pull
on Twinkle's mouth."
Maggie checks Emma's stirrups
and shortens them.

Walk

Trot

When Emma hears her name called,
she squeezes Twinkle's sides
to make him walk on.
At the signal to trot,
she shortens the reins a little
and sits up tall.
She gives him a gentle nudge
with her legs.
Finally, she uses a firm squeeze
with her legs to ask him to canter.
"Good job, Emma!" says Maggie.
"You did very well."
"Good job, Twinkle!"
says Emma.

Lucy and Lady take part
in the gymkhana.
These are races and games
on horseback.
The riders lead their horses
in the egg and spoon race.
Lady must not bump into Lucy.
If she does, the egg will fall
off the spoon.

Next comes the flag race.
Lucy leans to pick up the flag
and races to put it
in the flag holder.

Finally, it's time for
the bending event.
The horses weave in and out
between a line of poles.
They must not touch the poles.
Lucy is lucky to have
such a good horse.
They come second
and win a rosette.
"Good job, Lady."

Tom is nervous
about the jumping event.
Candy is twitching.
Her ears are back,
which is not a good sign.
Tom talks to her to calm her down.
"It's our turn next," he says.

As they trot into the ring
Candy's ears perk up.
She loves jumping
and can't wait to begin.
At last Tom can relax.
The first jump is big,
but Candy sails smoothly over it.
She is very calm now,
enjoying every minute of it.

Tom is thrilled
when he hears
it is a clear round.
"You were brilliant!"
calls Maggie.

Horse Blanket

A sweating horse is covered with a blanket to prevent it from cooling down too quickly and getting a chill.

The horses are hot and tired
after their hard work.
They have a drink of water
and eat some hay.
The children wash and brush them
before putting their blankets on.

Lucy, Emma, and Tom
have all won ribbons.
Tom is especially pleased.
He has a red rosette because
he and Candy won first prize
in their event.
"You're a star, Candy," he says.

Back at the stables,
the children watch their horses
grazing in the field.
But before they go home,
Tom has one last thing to do.
Poor old Bingo
missed all the fun today.

Tom gives him a pat
and strokes his nose.
"Don't worry, Bingo," says Tom.
"The vet says
you'll be better very soon.
We'll take you with us
next time."

Horse and Pony Breeds

There are many different breeds, or types, of horse and pony but all ponies are smaller than horses – 15 hands (a hand is four inches) is the limit for a full-grown pony.

The *Shetland* is the smallest type of pony, but it is also almost the strongest. Because of their size, Shetlands are mainly used to carry young children.

The *New Forest,* named after the British forest in which it is found, is a sturdy pony, up to 14 hands tall. Although not as pretty as the Welsh Mountain, it is good to ride and easy to manage.

The *Welsh Mountain* is the next smallest pony after the Shetland. Very pretty, the main colors are brown, gray, and chestnut.

The *Pinto,* or painted horse or pony, is white with either brown or black markings. Pintos are found all over the world.